D0403041

Take a Walk, JOHNNY

SISKIYOU CO. SUPT SCHOOLS
LIBRARY
609 S GOLD ST
YREKA, CA 96097

Margaret Hillert

Illustrated by Yoshi Miyake

MODERN CURRICULUM PRESS
Cleveland · Toronto

Text copyright © 1981 by Margaret Hillert. Illustrations and cover design copyright © 1981 by Modern Curriculum Press. Original illustration and cover design copyright © 1981 by Follett Publishing Company. All rights reserved. Printed in the United States of America. This book or parts thereof may not be reproduced in any form or mechanically stored in any retrieval system without written permission of the publisher.

Library of Congress Cataloging in Publication Data

Hillert, Margaret.
  Take a walk, Johnny.

Summary: Johnny's summer morning walks, taken initially from boredom, become quite adventurous.
I. Miyake, Yoshi.   II. Title.
PZ7.H558Tak   (E)   81-4044   AACR2

ISBN 0-8136-5611-7 (Paperback)

ISBN 0-8136-5111-5 (Hardbound)

    15 16 17 18 19 20   99

During the school year Johnny got up early
every morning. He ate a good breakfast
and got dressed. Then he made his bed,
cleaned up his room, and went off to
school with his friends.

When summer came, school was out. Johnny got up early on the first day of summer. He ate a good breakfast and got dressed. Then he made his bed, cleaned up his room, and looked for something to do.

First Johnny played with his toy cars. Then he made silly faces in the mirror and laughed to see himself.

Next Johnny looked at the plants that were growing in the glass box on the table.

After that he went to his mother and said, "Mother, what can I do now? I don't have anything to do."

Mother said, "Take a walk, Johnny."

So Johnny went out to the yard and walked around. He saw a bird up in a tree. He saw a butterfly on a flower. Then, under the flowers, he saw a big, brown toad.

"Hello, toad!" said Johnny. "What a good find you are! You have lots of bumps and funny eyes. Don't jump away, toad. I want to take you into the house and show you to Mother. She'll be surprised!"

Johnny went into the house. "Mother, look
at this toad!" he said. "Isn't he great?"

"Yes," said Mother. "He's a fine-looking
toad. Why don't you put him into your
glass box with the plants? That would
be a good place for him."

9

The next morning Johnny made his bed, cleaned up his room, and looked for something to do.

First he fed the toad. Then he took the toad out of the box and let him hop around the room.

After that Johnny went to his mother and said, "Mother, what can I do now? I don't have anything to do."

Mother said, "Take a walk, Johnny."

Johnny went out to the yard with his toad. He put the toad back under the flowers.

"Good-bye, toad," said Johnny. "You'll be happier here."

Johnny walked down the sidewalk and looked all around. "I wonder what I'll find today," he said.

Then, under a tree, he saw a rock.

"What a pretty rock," said Johnny. "It has red and white spots, and it even seems to shine a little. I'll take it home and put it with my other rocks."

Johnny went back to his house. "Mother, look at this rock!" he said.

"It's a beautiful rock," said Mother. "I'm glad you found it. You can put it with your other rocks."

The next morning Johnny made his bed, cleaned up his room, and looked for something to do.

First he took out all his rocks. Then he put them all back in boxes again.

After that Johnny went to his mother and said, "Mother, what can I do now? I don't have anything to do."

Mother said, "Take a walk, Johnny."

Johnny went outside. "Take a walk. Take a walk," he said. "That's all I ever seem to do. But this time I know where I'll go."

Johnny walked to the library.

"Just look at all the books," he said. "I can
get a book about almost anything. There
are books about cowboys and wagons, bridges
and mountains, and elephants and circuses.
What a wonderful place this is!"

Johnny picked out some books and took
them home. "Look here, Mother," he said.
"I like to read, and these books are full of
good things to read about."

"I see you went to the library," said
Mother. "What a good idea! Books are
fun to read, and it looks like you found
some good ones."

The next morning Johnny made his bed, cleaned up his room, and looked for something to do.

He read for a time. Then he put all his books away.

After that Johnny went to his mother and said, "Mother, what can I do now? I don't have anything to do."

Mother said, "Take a walk, Johnny."

Johnny went outside and began to walk. "Walk, walk, walk," he said. "I'm getting tired of all this walking."

Suddenly he saw something shiny on the sidewalk. "What's this?" he said. "It's money right here on the sidewalk! Now I can **run** to the ice cream store."

So Johnny ran to the ice cream store.

"Boy, what a great place!" he said.
"Just look at all the different kinds of
ice cream. There are so many kinds that
I don't know which one to pick."

"Take your time," said the man.

"The chocolate looks good," said Johnny
at last. "I would like a chocolate ice
cream cone."

Johnny ate his ice cream cone on the way home.

"Mother!" said Johnny. "Guess what I found on my walk this time. I found money! I found money, and I got an ice cream cone."

"You did?" said Mother. "The money was a good find, wasn't it?"

The next morning Johnny did all the same things. He ate breakfast. He made his bed. He cleaned up his room.

After that Johnny went to his mother and said, "Mother, I am going for a walk."

His mother said, "Have a good time, Johnny."

Johnny walked and walked and walked. He walked up and down. He walked around and around.

Suddenly Johnny saw a little puppy in the street. "Here, puppy. Here, puppy," he called.

But the puppy did not move out of the street.

Johnny looked both ways for cars. Then
he ran to get the puppy out of the street.

"Oh, you poor little thing," said Johnny.
"Don't you have a home? You must be lost.
I'll bet you need something to eat. Do
you want to come home with me? Maybe I
can keep you."

Johnny took the puppy home.

"Mother!" said Johnny. "Look what I found on my walk this time. She is so little. I think she is lost. May we keep her, Mother?"

"Well," said Mother. "First let's read the Lost and Found part of the newspaper."

Mother looked in the newspaper. "No, I don't see anything about a lost puppy in here," she said. "Now we will make some signs."

Johnny and his mother made signs. The signs looked like this.

They put one sign on a tree. They put another sign in the ice cream store. When they got home, the telephone rang.

"I see you found my puppy," said a man on the telephone. "You can have her. I can't take care of her."

Mother told Johnny what the man had said. "You can keep the puppy, Johnny," said Mother. "She's as cute as a button."

"Cute as a button. Cute as a button," said Johnny. "Oh, Mother. Button would be a nice name for her."

Then Johnny called to the puppy. "Here, Button. Here, Button. Now you are my puppy. We'll be such good friends."

Every morning after that, Johnny got up early and ate a good breakfast. Then he made his bed, cleaned up his room, and went for a walk with Button.

And sometimes Mother went walking
with them.

Margaret Hillert, author and poet, has written many books for young readers. She is a former first-grade teacher and lives in Birmingham, Michigan.

In addition to giving practice with words that most children will recognize, *Take a Walk, Johnny* uses the 35 enrichment words listed below.

breakfast	dressed	nice	shine
bridges	during		shiny
bumps		outside	sidewalk
butterfly	early		signs
button	elephants	plants	spots
		poor	suddenly
chocolate	ice		
circuses	idea	rang	telephone
cone		rock(s)	tired
cowboys	mirror		toad
cream			
cute			wonder
			wonderful